MW01130547

6 Days till SUNDAY

Knox Vestal

ISBN 978-1-63961-931-3 (paperback)
ISBN 978-1-63961-942-9 (hardcover)
ISBN 978-1-63961-932-0 (digital)

Christian Faith Publishing
832 Park Avenue
Meadville, PA 16335
www.christianfaithpublishing.com

Printed in the United States of America

To the memory of my nana Pat Vestal,
who passed away on November 7, 2018,
after battling cancer for five years.
My nana was a strong woman who loved her family very much.
I miss her, but I know I will someday see her again.
I love you, Nana.

To my big brother, Jack.
Like all brothers, we sometimes don't get along. But
I know Jack loves me, and I know I love him.
I really look up to my brother.

CONTENTS

ACKNOWLEDGMENTS

I want to thank my grandpa Steve Morrow for encouraging me to write this book and for helping me get it done.

I also want to thank all of my family for their support. I'm not sure about our dog, but everyone else was 100 percent behind me.

I want to thank all my teachers at school and at church for helping me learn about important things.

I want to thank my friends for always having my back.

But most of all, I want to glorify God and thank Him for giving me a new life through His son, Jesus.

INTRODUCTION FOR PARENTS AND GRANDPARENTS

Through my years as a grandfather, I've been blessed to have experienced some very special times with each of my five grandchildren. I truly believe that children and grandchildren are treasures from above. Now before you are tempted to dismiss this as "grandpa talk," you might want to check out what the Bible has to say in Psalm 127:3.

Not only have Jack, Annie, Sophie, Alex, Knox, and I been able to make some lasting memories, I like to think that God has perhaps used my life to somehow contribute to theirs. I do know this: My grandkids continue to enrich my life beyond any words I can say.

When Knox (now eleven) and I (now sixty-nine) first started talking about this book project, I was impressed by his sincerity, so I decided to encourage him. I wanted him to know that his idea for a book could possibly become a reality. And if memory serves me right, he responded with typical Knoxspeak: "Seriously?"

This book is not my book. It is Knox's book. He is the author, and I am the author's helper. From time to time, I may have tweaked it a bit when necessary, but he owns the text. The expressed words and feelings are his. It is Knox's hope that this book will be able to help other children who are seeking to know God's plan for their lives.

It pleases me to provide the introduction for *6 Days till Sunday*. I pray that it will be a beneficial resource for children's ministers, Sunday school teachers, parents, grandparents, and children alike. God bless.

Steve Morrow

K
HOLY
BIBLE

CHAPTER 1

Which Way?

Hi! My name is Knox Vestal. I am eleven years old, and this is my story. But wait. The best parts of my story can be like the best parts of your story too, so let's get started.

When I was seven years old, I made a very important decision about my life. Looking back on it, I believe it was the most important decision I have ever made. Really!

I knew in my heart that I needed to make a choice. I'm not talking about something like choosing between a cherry slush and a frozen limeade. No, the choice I was facing was much more important than that. And here's the thing: nobody else would be able to make this choice for me, not even my parents.

You see, I had to decide which way I wanted to live my life. If I chose my way, I would pay no attention to God and His plan for my life. If I chose God's way, I would become a Christian by believing God sent His son, Jesus, to pay the price for everyone's sins. As a believer, I will someday go to heaven, and I will live with our awesome God, His son, Jesus, and other believers forever! That's amazing! The same thing can happen to you. You can look it up for yourself in John 3:16 of your Bible.

This is how it all started for me. One evening, I walked into the kitchen of our house where my mom was cooking supper. I remember it was dark outside. "Hey, Mom," I said. "What's for supper!" Then, before she even had time to answer, I blurted out another question. "Mom, how do I become a Christian?"

Mom smiled. I remember her answer was all about God's love for me and how God sent His son, Jesus, to die on the cross for my sins and then come alive again.

Sin happens when we disobey God. We are all sinners. But here is the good news. If we pray and tell God we are sorry for our sins, and that we believe He sent Jesus to save us from our sins, then God forgives our sins! How cool is that? You see, we cannot save ourselves. It can only happen when we trust in Jesus as our Lord and Savior. Wowza!

That night, I went to bed knowing it was time to make my decision. I'm so glad I chose God's way over my way. Now my old life is gone, and I have a new life with Jesus as my Savior, Leader, and Guide. What about you?

CHAPTER 2

Tuesday Thoughts

Soon after I became a Christian, I noticed other things started to fall into place. Three of these are listed below.

- I made a profession of faith. This happened when I came forward in my church to let people know I had become a Christian.
- I took part in the "new Christian" class, where I learned a lot about what it means to be a follower of Jesus.
- But the thing I was most excited about was counting down the days until the day of my baptism. I remembered watching my cousin Alex get baptized. I cried tears of joy because I was so happy for Alex. This time, I'll be happy for me!

K

The Bible tells us the meaning of baptism in Romans 6:4. In this verse, Jesus is referred to as Christ. By getting baptized, I will be showing others how my old life has been replaced by what the Bible calls *newness of life*.

With each new day, I kept thinking about God and His love for me. I mean, God loves me so much that He gave me the best gift ever—Jesus. And He wants to do the same for you. That is so awesome!

Heavenly Blessings

Earthly Blessing

Even though I was a young boy, I could tell that Jesus had changed my life. By getting baptized, I would be able to show others a picture of what had already taken place in my life.

I knew God wanted me to obey Him and be baptized. I just kept wishing that the big day would hurry up and get here.

Then, it hit me. It was Tuesday. Let's see: Tuesday, Wednesday, Thursday, Friday, Saturday, Sunday. The day of my baptism was only six days away!

CHAPTER 3

God Loves You and Me

I could hardly wait for Sunday to arrive. But here's the thing: I didn't have to wait until Sunday to start living my life as a Christian.

I was so thankful for God's love. I mean, just think about it. You and I are loved by our families, our friends, and even our pets! But God's love for us is even greater than that.

There is something very special about the love of God. He washes away our sins if we believe in Jesus, and He provides a place in heaven so that we can live forever. Now that is big-time love!

But God doesn't just forget about us while we go on living here on earth. As Christians, we can walk with Jesus, talk with Jesus, and live for Jesus. At first, I didn't completely understand all of this, but now I'm beginning to get it, but I know I still have a lot to learn!

There are many Bible verses that tell us how we can follow Jesus by living out God's love in our daily lives. Three of these are listed below.

- In 1 John 4:19, we are told that our ability to love comes from God's love for us.
- The two greatest commands of Jesus are all about love. You can find them in Mark 12:30–31.

- We can see what love looks like by reading 1 Corinthians 13:4–5 and then doing what it says.

> We love each other because he loved us first. (1 John 4:19 NLT)
>
> And you must love the Lord your God with all your heart, all your soul, all your mind, and all your strength. The second is equally important: "Love your neighbor as yourself." No other commandment is greater than these. (Mark 12:30–31 NLT)
>
> Love is patient and kind. Love is not jealous or boastful or proud or rude. It does not demand its own way. It is not irritable, and it keeps no record of being wronged. (1 Corinthians 13:4–5 NLT)

God is love, and the New Testament of the Bible is filled with examples of Jesus showing us how to love. Do you know that the Bible is kind of like an onion (this is what my mom says)? You know how an onion has lots of layers? She's always saying that each time we read the Bible, we peel back more and more layers of truth. Pretty cool, huh?

MILK

CHAPTER 4

God Is with You and Me

Have you ever felt like you were all alone? Yes, I know this happened to the boy in the movie *Home Alone*, but that's another story. Here are two examples of what I'm talking about.

- It was the first day of school, and my stomach didn't feel right. Grown-ups call this stress, but I call it a bad case of the "butterflies." When I walked into my new class, I felt pretty much alone with just my thoughts and questions. Will I like my new teacher? Will my new teacher like me? Will there be any bullies in my class? Will I like the cafeteria food? Well, if I don't like the food, I guess I could start taking my own lunch to school—duh. But here's the thing, whether you or I are homeschooled or attend a public or private school, we are probably going to feel alone at one time or another.

- I like to go camping with my dad, but how would it feel to be left alone in my tent overnight? I mean, what if Bigfoot decided to show up? Now that would *not* be a good time to be alone! It hasn't happened yet, but I'm always glad to have my dad there with me—just in case. Now, just so you know, I think Bigfoot may be more imaginary than real. But at least he helped me make my point!

Okay, so where do you think I'm going with this? The answer to this question is coming, but I'm guessing you may have already figured it out for yourself.

After Jesus died on the cross for our sins and came alive again, He met with His disciples (His followers) to give them their instructions. As a current-day follower of Jesus, I also need to follow His instructions. Matthew 28:16–20 is known as the Great Commission. I think it is a good idea for all Christians to memorize these verses so they will be ready, willing, and able to carry out the instructions of Jesus. In the very last sentence of verse 20, Jesus promises to always be with His followers. As a Christian and follower of Jesus, I know I can count on Him to never leave me all alone. Counting on Jesus means I have complete faith in Him. No matter what comes my way, I will always trust in Jesus.

> Then the eleven disciples left for Galilee, going to the mountain where Jesus had told them to go. When they saw him, they worshiped him—but some of them doubted!
>
> Jesus came and told his disciples, "I have been given all authority in heaven and on earth. Therefore, go and make disciples of all the nations, baptizing them in the name of the Father and the Son and the Holy Spirit. Teach these new disciples to obey all the commands I have given you. And be sure of this: I am with you always, even to the end of the age." (Matthew 28:16–20 NLT)

CHAPTER 5

Don't Be Afraid

With Jesus in my heart, I do not have to be afraid. But it wasn't always that way.

I used to be afraid of the dark. I mean, I was sometimes afraid even when the night-light was on in my room. Seriously! But all of that is behind me now.

Another thing I used to be afraid of was being separated from my family. I remember sitting by my mom in church one day. I had something on my mind. I was trying to keep quiet, but then I decided to whisper something to my mom. “I don’t want to go to heaven. I just want to stay here.” I think I was just scared because I didn’t want to be away from my parents and my brother and sister. Later, Mom told me everything was going to be okay because every person who believes in Jesus will someday live in heaven, including all of our family. Mom’s words made me feel much better.

The day of my baptism was getting closer and closer. I admit I was a little nervous about being up in front of a lot of people. But then, as He always does, Jesus calmed my fear.

K

CHAPTER 6

Getting Ready

On the day before my baptism, a lot of questions were rolling around in my head. Will my parents be near me when Pastor Rich lowers me into the water and raises me back up? Will water get in my nose? Will the water be cold? Will other people from my family be there to watch me get baptized? Will I get ice cream?

Other thoughts were also on my mind. And with this being a Saturday, I had plenty of time to think!

I thought about my own family and their words of encouragement. By the way, my parents and my brother and sister have certain words they just like to say. Is it like that in your family too? For example, my dad likes to say, "Are you sure?" My mom always has to get us going. She likes to say, "Is everybody ready?" My brother, Jack, likes to say "Hey," and my sister, Sophie, is always saying, "Wait, what?" I guess I should also tell you that one of my main words is "Seriously?" But now, back to my Saturday thoughts.

I thought about my grandparents and how happy they were that I was getting baptized on Sunday. I knew all four of them would be there with smiles on their faces and tears in their eyes.

I thought about my friends and teachers. I had already told them I was getting baptized on Sunday. Part of getting ready for Sunday was telling these people about this special day in my life.

And, of course, I thought about God because He made all of this possible when He sent His son, Jesus, to die on the cross for my sins and then come alive again. You know, baptism doesn't make you a Christian, but when we get baptized, we are obeying Jesus and showing others a picture of what is happening in our lives when we become a Christian. Did you know Jesus Himself was baptized? When we get baptized, we are also following Jesus's example. Tomorrow I'll be letting people know that Jesus is alive and I'm living for Him! Let's go!

CHAPTER 7

Sunday!

When I woke up this morning, I was very excited. The last day of the countdown was finally here.

After I got ready for church, my mom and dad told me they were proud of me. That made me feel really good. As of today, everyone in my family would be baptized followers of Jesus, and this too made me happy. But being a baptized believer in Jesus does not necessarily mean I will always be happy about everything that happens. It does mean I can always be happy that I am a Christian because life with Jesus is the best way to go.

When I got to church, I remember walking up to the place where I was going to get baptized. My grandpa was there to help me get ready. I also remember that Grandpa was the first person I saw when I came out of the baptistery.

A baptistery looks like a small swimming pool. But don't worry, I didn't dive in. And just in case you are wondering, you don't have to get baptized in a baptistery. It can happen in a big washtub or even in a lake or creek, or maybe even a swimming pool!

I remember listening to my dad as he read my testimony to everyone who was there. My testimony described how I became a Christian.

I remember the words of Pastor Rich when he lowered me into the water and then raised me back up: “Buried with Christ (Jesus) in baptism, raised to walk in newness of life.” These were the words I had been waiting to hear. Woo-hoo!

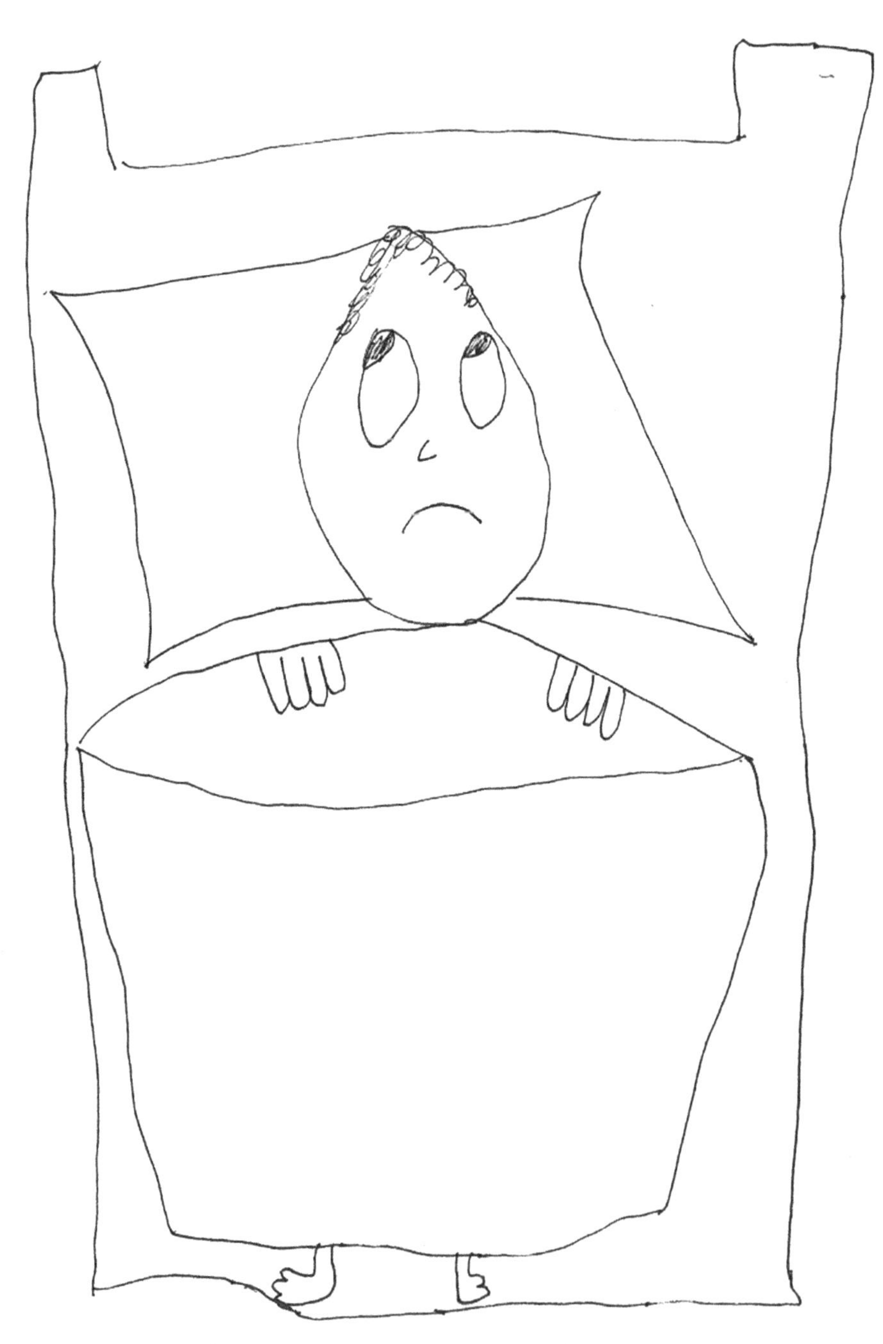

I used to be afraid of the dark.

So many questions.

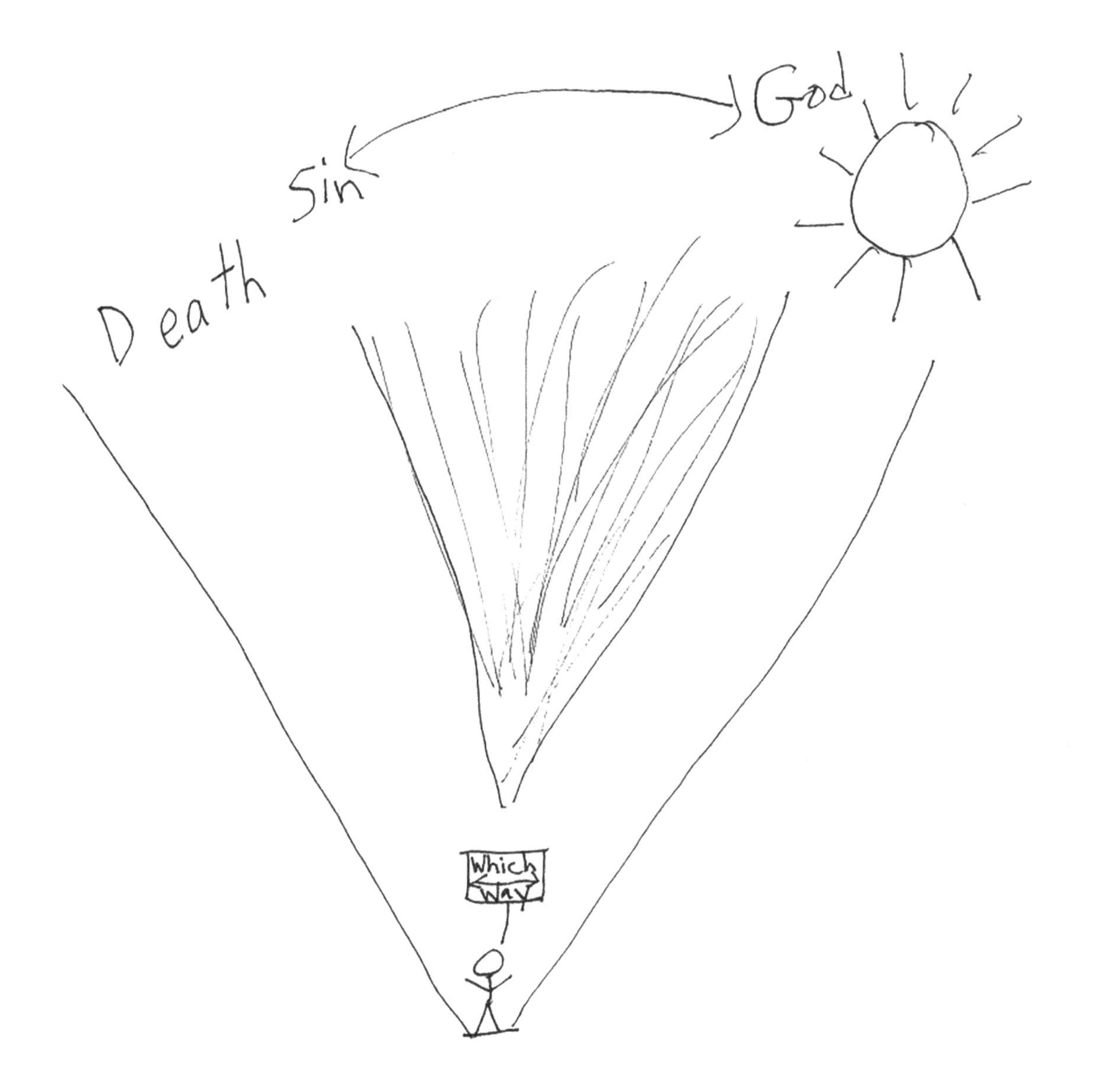

God's way is the best way.

Grandpa and me before my baptism.

Mom and Dad and me before my baptism.

Mom, Dad, Jack, Sophie, and me on vacation.

With my cousin Alex.

With my brother and sister.

Grandpa and me after a hard-fought game.

Top photo: Dad and me on a cold soccer day.
Bottom photo: Movin' and groovin'!

Thank you for reading my book! May God bless you always.

Knox Vestal

ABOUT THE AUTHOR

Knox Vestal is an eleven-year-old boy who was born in Bolivar, Missouri.

He is a fifth-grade student at Bolivar Intermediate School and a member of First Baptist Church in Bolivar.

Knox has several likes. He likes to make things. He likes soccer. His favorite subject in school is science. He enjoys reading the Wimpy Kid books. He likes table games, and he especially likes to win. Oh, and he likes to dance. He is particularly good at doing the moonwalk.

Knox came to know Jesus as his savior at the age of seven. Today he lives with his parents, Brady and Missy Vestal; his brother, Jack; his sister, Sophie; and the family dogs, a Boston terrier named Babbs and a boxer named Bo.

CPSIA information can be obtained
at www.ICGtesting.com
Printed in the USA
LVHW070745280622
722264LV00003B/28